AM🐝RA'S GARDEN ADVENTURE

Written by Aisha Belluccia

For permission requests, write to the publisher, addressed "Attention: Permissions Coordinator," 205 N. Michigan Avenue, Suite #810, Chicago, IL 60601. 13th & Joan books may be purchased for educational, business or sales promotional use. For information, bookdistribution@13thandjoan.com

Printed in the U. S. A.

First Printing, Copyright © 2023 by Aisha Belluccia.

ISBN: 978-1-953156-86-0

Amora's Garden Adventure introduces young kids and families to gardening through a fun story about hard work and patience, granting the sweetest reward.

Growing Everyday

My students loved every minute of reading *Amora's Garden Adventure*. Children love handson learning activities so this book has been added to my lesson plans. The students were able to follow along with Amora and grow plants of their own. In the story we are able to see the life cycle of a plant from seed to fruit, which was a fulfilling experience.

Amy Curtner

Educator

Dedication

In loving memory of a writer, mom, sister,
and best friend, who will continue to inspire
many beyond time and space.
You are born whole.

Love You Abi

Epigraph

To nurture our youth is to invest in the future.

-Rose Brown
Early childhood educator

In this story you will peek into Amora's grandma's backyard, a lush and green tropical oasis full of wonder and mystery.

Adventure with Amora as she discovers just how much it takes to create yummy fruits and vegetables.

Ready! Set! Grow!

Table of Contents

Preface

Seed, soil, sun, and water! Anything can grow
as big as you can imagine it when you nurture it.
Amora gets that warm fuzzy feeling when
the seed pops out of the soil and stretches
its leaves toward the sun.

It is her job to water it and make sure it gets
everything a plant needs. The higher it grows, the
better she feels.

Amora has everything she needs to start right now.

Ready! Set! Grow!

A Message From the Author

I decided to write this book because I want kids to know where their food comes from so they can make healthier choices growing into adulthood. Children are curious learners and love handson activities. Growing plants allows kids to discover fruits and vegetables through a new lens. Tomatoes on a dinner plate often get overlooked, but a fresh one picked from the vine tastes so much sweeter. My goal for writing this story is to encourage my community to make healthier choices. If a child, or even an adult, were to try new fruits and vegetables or explore the wonders of gardening as a result of reading this book, then my job has been accomplished.

Aisha

Amora loves visiting her grandma's house, it is a magical place. When she walks into the backyard, all the loud city noises become calm.

Car horns and emergency sirens are drowned out by a canopy of swaying tropical fruit trees.

It is amazing how a small backyard garden can feel like acres of rolling hills in the countryside.
This is her happy place.

Sometimes Amora imagines herself as a tree, as tall as she can be. Her arms are palm leaves stretched way out high, swaying in the breeze. Her tall, full hair is fashioned like a rose bush.

Sprinkling the plants with water
is Amora's favorite thing to do.
She knows plants need plenty
of water to grow and lots
of sunlight too. Walking in the garden,
Amora spots all the little bugs.
A ladybug on a leaf and a worm
crawling in the mud.

Amora wants to plant a little mango tree.
Her grandma shows her how to grow this plant
from just a little seed. First she will dig a tiny hole,
then put the sprout in the ground so it can...

Ready! Set! Grow!

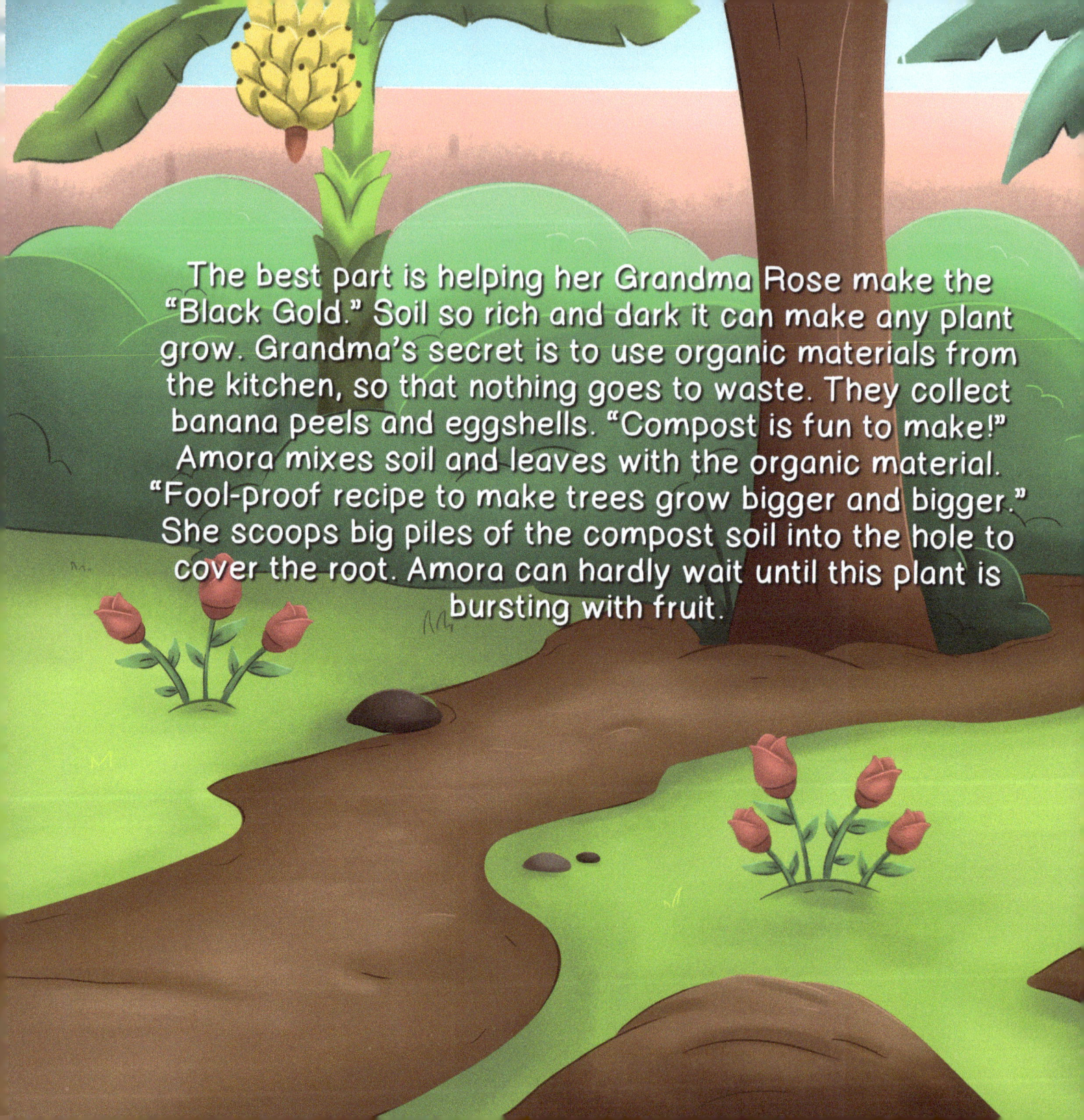

The best part is helping her Grandma Rose make the "Black Gold." Soil so rich and dark it can make any plant grow. Grandma's secret is to use organic materials from the kitchen, so that nothing goes to waste. They collect banana peels and eggshells. "Compost is fun to make!" Amora mixes soil and leaves with the organic material. "Fool-proof recipe to make trees grow bigger and bigger." She scoops big piles of the compost soil into the hole to cover the root. Amora can hardly wait until this plant is bursting with fruit.

Every morning Amora goes outside to water her tree. She measures herself, "It is almost as tall as me!" As Amora enjoys the birds whistling their early tunes, she cannot help but dream of all the juicy mango fruit her tree will produce. Amora watches over her plant for an hour each day.

She spots another creature who wants to eat her tree, "No, go away!" Amora knows what to do right away. She escorts the hungry caterpillars off the leaves and invites the helpful ladybugs to stay.

Little volcanoes come as a surprise! Her tree grows right before her very eyes. Amora is amazed to see how tall her tree has grown. In a month there are new limbs sprouting all on their own. Amora smiles every time she sees her tree.

Like magic, her hard work has come to life. She is so obsessed, she even counts every new leaf twice! Amora decides to keep a journal of her plants' progress. She closely observes and even draws pictures of all the insects.

The next month, Amora sees beautiful red and white blossoms spring from the branches. She realizes a wonderful thing. She knows these blossoms will bloom into small fruit.

She is so happy that she begins to sing. The roots run deeper as the branches get taller and thicker. They have to support the weight of the mangoes as they get heavier and bigger.

Amora's grandma told her she would be able to eat the mangoes when they are ripe. That was great motivation. Amora cared for the tree for six months straight, she understands that growing takes patience. The mango fruit started off green in color, then slowly turned to red and orange. It was quite a sight to see, like leaves changing color in a forest.

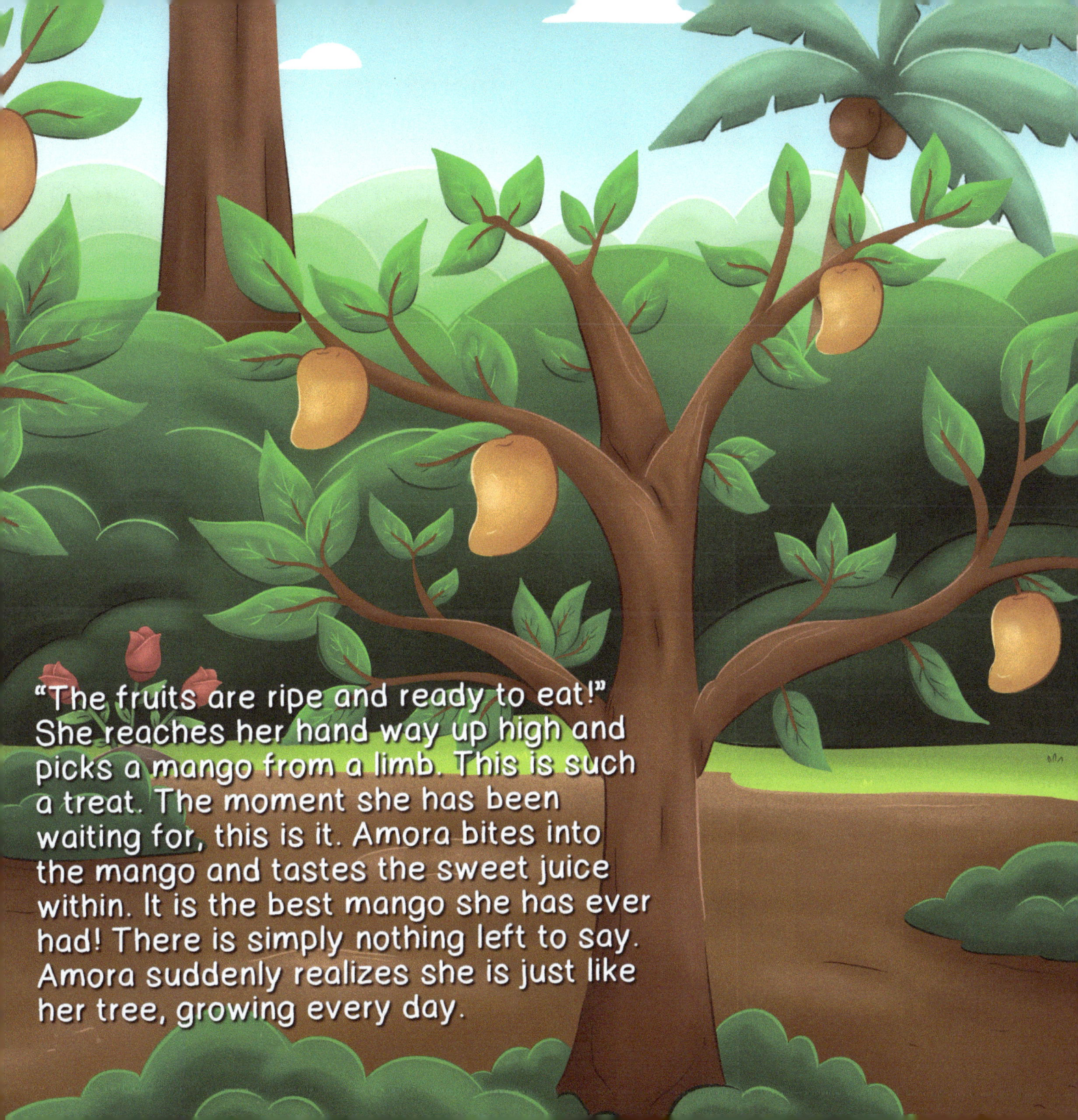

"The fruits are ripe and ready to eat!"
She reaches her hand way up high and
picks a mango from a limb. This is such
a treat. The moment she has been
waiting for, this is it. Amora bites into
the mango and tastes the sweet juice
within. It is the best mango she has ever
had! There is simply nothing left to say.
Amora suddenly realizes she is just like
her tree, growing every day.

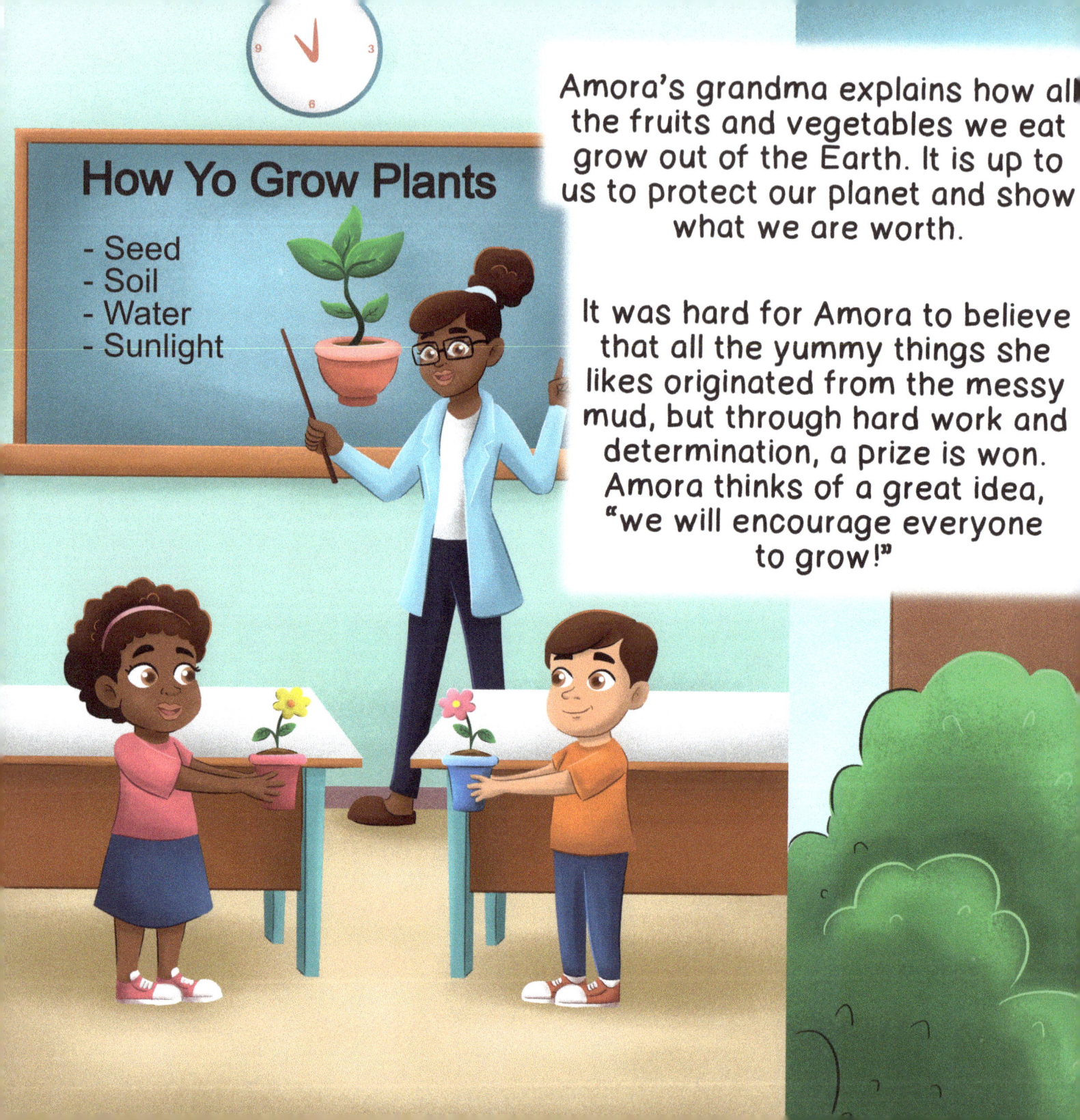

Amora's grandma explains how all the fruits and vegetables we eat grow out of the Earth. It is up to us to protect our planet and show what we are worth.

It was hard for Amora to believe that all the yummy things she likes originated from the messy mud, but through hard work and determination, a prize is won. Amora thinks of a great idea, "we will encourage everyone to grow!"

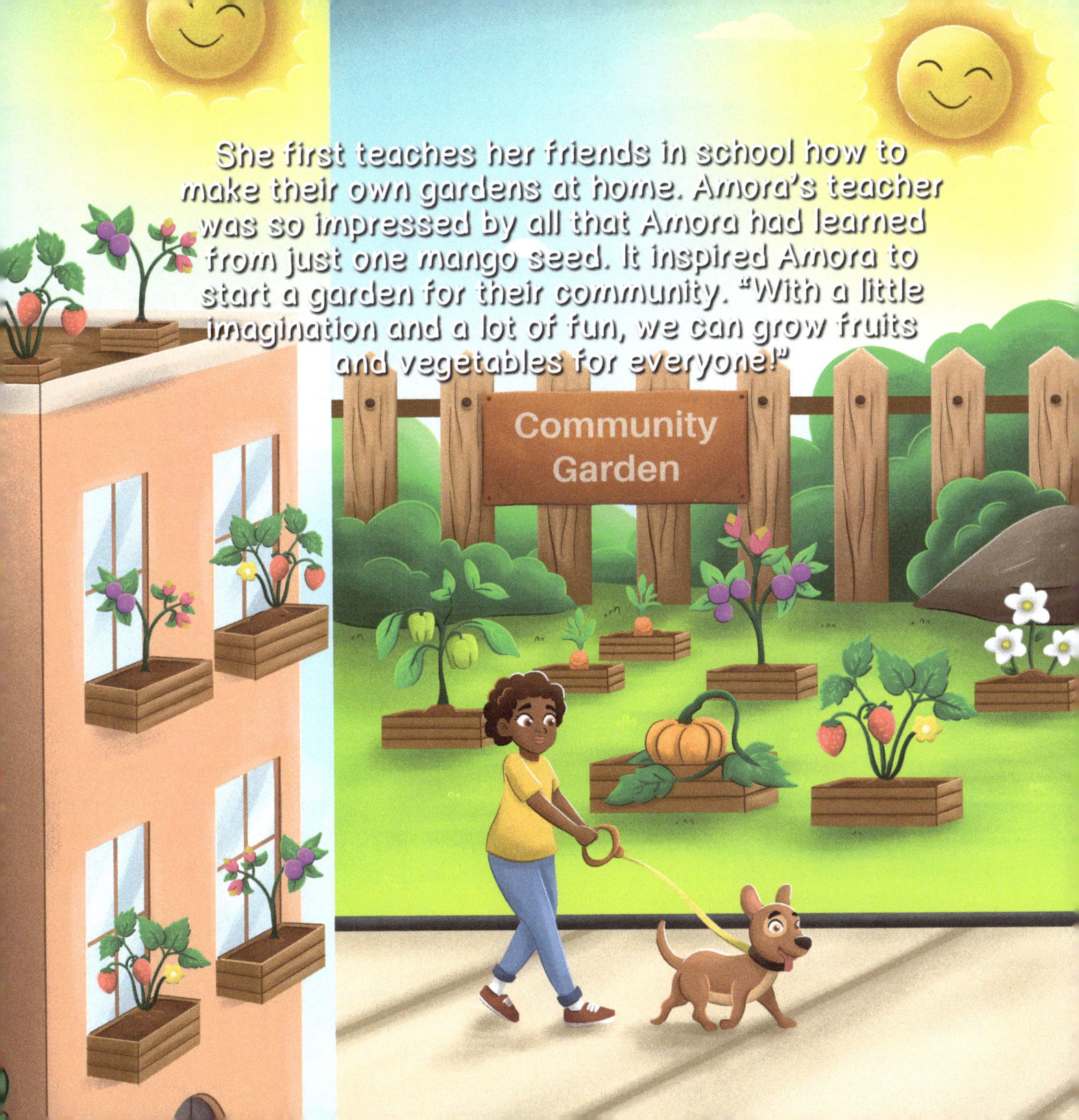

She first teaches her friends in school how to make their own gardens at home. Amora's teacher was so impressed by all that Amora had learned from just one mango seed. It inspired Amora to start a garden for their community. "With a little imagination and a lot of fun, we can grow fruits and vegetables for everyone!"

Community Garden

Tools to Grow

How can you help protect the planet?

Participate in trash pickup with family and friends to clean up the neighborhood. Always recycle.

Start your own garden at home, school, or in your community. It will be hard work, but you can do it. Start growing and sharing tasty fruits and vegetables.

Where do mangoes grow best?

Mango trees grow best in tropical climates where it is warm and rains often.

How long does
it take a mango tree to produce fruit?

2-3 years.

Use a journal as a tool to write
the details of your plant growth.

What are some helpful insects in the garden?

How do pollinators help plants?

Ladybugs, bees, and butterflies are just
a few garden friends. These insects spread
pollen from plant to plant, which helps to
create new plants.

Some plants like: strawberry, blackberry, and raspberry, only take a few months to mature. While other trees like mango, orange, and apple may take years to develop fruit.

Helpful tools to use while gardening: shovel, gloves, watering can, seeds, clear ground or pot with soil, and compost.

What is your favorite fruit or vegetable?

Most important tip:

Be a friend to nature.

Conclusion

Amora realizes that as the plant grows a little everyday, she grows with it. Each new leaf brings a brand new discovery. The lessons she learns from going on this journey has improved her patience and helped her curate a love for gardening just like her Grandmother. Amora has learned so much and wants to share her knowledge with everyone she knows.

Epilogue

Seed, soil, sun, and water come together to create magic. Nature has already provided the materials we need. Growing plants gives everyone a sense of purpose and belonging that connects us all to this great Earth. Make Earth Day everyday.

Sheajah Mcpherson

Community Advocate, Entrepreneur

Acknowledgments

This book was written for Leekari, Janiyah, Zakyla, Aiden, Irie, Jahkai, Haile, Zaire, Azura, and Kaia. With patience, knowledge, and a gentle hand, anything can be created. Your lives encourage me to keep growing.

About the Author

Aisha Belluccia is an animal scientist who loves all things outdoors. The fresh air and bright sunshine bring her inspiration. This story is close to her heart as it is the story of how she fell in love with nature. Growing up in a big city there are not many open spaces to grow plants, but she learned early on that a balcony ledge with a lot of sunshine would do just fine. Aisha's Jamaican heritage plays a big part in her love for tropical fruits, such as mangos, and she often ate them as a child. Mangos were her mother and grandmothers' favorite fruit. They were the ones who passed down their green thumb to Aisha. Now Aisha knows the secret to make any plant grow, and she intends to share it with you.
All it takes is soil, water, sunlight, and a little bit of love.

Author's social media

Instagram: GrowingEveryday2020

Facebook: Aisha AllSmiles Belluccia

www.ingramcontent.com/pod-product-compliance
Lightning Source LLC
Chambersburg PA
CBHW041526120626

46551CB00018B/2592